CONTENTS

Copyright Page	1
Preamble	2
Chapter 1: The Lost Art of the Generalist	4
Chapter 2: The Search for the Fixer	6
Chapter 3: T.E.A.L.	9
Chapter 4: Your Leadership Style	15
Chapter 5: Decentralized Learning Theory	19
Chapter 6: 0 to 100	24
Chapter 7: Perception	28
Chapter 8: The Big Picture	33
Chapter 9: Blueprints to Scale	37
Chapter 10: Precious Resource	42
Chapter 11: Navigating Digital Transformation	47
Chapter 12: Inclusive Leadership and the Power of Diversity	49
Chapter 13: Leading in Remote and Hybrid Work Environments	51
Chapter 14: Managing Mental Health and Well-Being	53
Chapter 15: Sustainability and Ethical Leadership	55
Chapter 16: Agile Leadership and Adaptability	58
Chapter 17: Blueprints to Start	61
Chapter 18: Becoming the Ultimate Fixer	66

References 72
About the Author 83

COPYRIGHT PAGE

While every precaution has been taken in the preparation of this book, the publisher assumes no responsibility for errors or omissions, or for damages resulting from the use of the information contained herein.

BECOMING A FIXER

First edition. October 1, 2024.

Copyright © 2024 Teivian.

Written by Teivian.

PREAMBLE

Welcome to **"Becoming a Fixer"**—a transformative journey into mastering the art and science of being a Fixer. I'm Teivian, your guide and the author of this book. Over the years, I've taken on the role of a Fixer in nearly every organisation I've worked with. This path has led me to a highly rewarding career, and now, I'm here to show you how you can join the ranks of the **Elite Fixers Club**.

When I first started, I joined a government entity where I quickly realized that unconventional thinking and radical work ethics were not the norms. In that environment, success was often measured by how well you conformed—how you dressed, how you presented yourself, and how closely you adhered to established practices. It didn't take long—just six months—for me to recognize that this wasn't where I would thrive. So, I moved on, seeking a role that would allow me to grow both personally and professionally.

My next step was in the e-learning industry, where I began developing many of the skills that I'll share with you in this book. These experiences laid the groundwork for my evolution into a Fixer. A few years later, I was headhunted for a management consulting role, which eventually led me to the professional training industry in a similar capacity. Most recently, I've been running projects for a tech company. Across all these roles, one thing remained constant: I was brought in to solve problems and interact with people at every level, from entry-level employees to the C-suite.

In these roles, I had to be knowledgeable, influential, and above all, an exceptional problem-solver.

This book is more than just a guide—it's a blueprint for those who aspire to become versatile problem-solvers. It's for individuals who can step into any situation, quickly assess what needs to be done, and drive meaningful change. Whether you're looking to apply these principles in your personal life or professional career, the insights here are universally applicable.

In the chapters that follow, we'll delve into the concepts, methodologies, and frameworks that will help you master the skills necessary to thrive in today's dynamic and unpredictable world. These are the same principles I've cultivated throughout my career as a Fixer.

As we begin, I encourage you to keep an open mind. Becoming a Fixer isn't just about learning specific skills; it's about adopting the right mindset. Throughout this book, I'll challenge conventional thinking and encourage you to approach problems from fresh perspectives. Now, let's dive in and explore what it truly means to be a Fixer in today's world.

CHAPTER 1: THE LOST ART OF THE GENERALIST

The Fixer is often seen as "a jack of all trades, master of none." But in today's fast-paced world, this phrase should be redefined. A Fixer is someone who combines broad knowledge with the ability to adapt and excel in diverse situations—a skillset that is increasingly rare and valuable.

In the past, when companies were smaller and more agile, employees often wore multiple hats. These generalists were crucial in helping organisations grow and navigate challenges. However, as industries evolved, the focus shifted toward specialization. The market demanded experts who could push the envelope in specific fields, leading to a workforce filled with highly specialized professionals.

While specialization brought about innovation and efficiency, it also introduced new challenges. organisations began to over-hire during boom periods, only to face the painful reality of layoffs during economic downturns. Specialists, while indispensable in their fields, often found themselves vulnerable to changing market conditions and technological disruptions.

This brings us to the concept of the Fixer—a modern-day generalist who thrives in a volatile, uncertain, complex, and ambiguous (VUCA) world. A Fixer is not limited by a single area of expertise. Instead, they bring a unique combination of skills, adaptability, and a fresh perspective to any situation. They are the ones who challenge the status quo, driving innovation across all fronts—whether it's marketing, operations, sales, or product development.

The value of a Fixer lies in their ability to see the big picture and connect the dots across various disciplines. They are the ones who can step in when the traditional playbook no longer works, offering creative solutions that others might overlook. In a world where agility and versatility are key to success, the Fixer is an asset that every organisation needs.

Fixers are individuals committed to driving change within an organisation from the inside out, leveraging their unique perspective and expertise to deliver results that matter.

CHAPTER 2: THE SEARCH FOR THE FIXER

Now that we've established the importance of a Fixer, the next logical question is: How do you become one? The answer is both simple and complex. Fixers aren't found through traditional hiring processes; they're often developed within an organisation by recognizing and nurturing certain traits.

The role of a Fixer doesn't come with a specific job title, but it closely aligns with roles like Operations Managers or Project Managers—positions that require a blend of strategic thinking, adaptability, and leadership. Let's explore how these roles can serve as the breeding ground for Fixers.

The Project Manager: The Visionary Executor

Project Managers are the backbone of any organisation. They oversee the execution of projects, ensuring that timelines are met, budgets are adhered to, and client expectations are exceeded. However, their role often extends beyond just managing tasks—they are the ones who must navigate the complexities of people management, resource allocation, and crisis resolution.

In many ways, Project Managers embody the spirit of a Fixer. They are not just specialists in their domain, but also have the unique ability to see the big picture and manage diverse teams making them invaluable. The best Project Managers are those who don't just stick to the script; they adapt, innovate, and find ways to deliver results even in the face of unexpected challenges.

However, once a project is completed, Project Managers often enter a phase of waiting—waiting for the next big project, the next challenge. This downtime can be an opportunity for organisations to harness their skills in other areas, encouraging them to take on Fixer roles that extend beyond the confines of project management.

The Operations Manager: The Guardian of Stability

While Project Managers are focused on the here and now, Operations Managers are the keepers of the status quo. Their job is to ensure that the organisation runs like a well-oiled machine, with processes and systems in place that guarantee efficiency and stability. However, this focus on maintaining the current state can sometimes make Operations Managers resistant to change.

The overlap between Operations Managers and Fixers occurs when stability becomes a barrier to growth. A Fixer, while respecting the need for order, knows when to disrupt the status quo to drive progress. They're the ones who can look at an existing process and identify opportunities for improvement through innovation, optimization, or a complete overhaul.

In essence, while Project Managers and Operations Managers might be the closest roles to a Fixer within an organisation, becoming a true Fixer requires more than just fulfilling these roles—it demands a mindset shift. It's about seeking out opportunities, embracing change, and being willing to step into the unknown to drive meaningful results.

So, where can you find a Fixer? Look within your own ranks. Identify those who aren't afraid to challenge the norm, who show an aptitude for learning and adapting, and who are driven by a desire to make a difference. These are the individuals who have the potential to become the Fixers the organisation needs.

CHAPTER 3: T.E.A.L.

The **Trust, Emotional Quotient, Action, Logic (T.E.A.L)** framework is crucial for the modern Fixer, serving as a guiding principle in every decision and action taken. Let's explore each component in detail.

Trust

Building Trust: The Foundation of Influence

Trust isn't merely about keeping promises or being honest; it's about creating a consistent track record that makes others feel secure in your abilities. As a Fixer, your role often involves stepping into chaotic or uncertain situations, where trust can be easily eroded if mishandled.

Steps to Build Trust:

- **Consistency in Delivery:** Always deliver what you promise, and if unforeseen circumstances arise, communicate promptly and transparently.
- **Openness and Vulnerability:** Don't be afraid to admit when you don't know something or when you've made a mistake. This transparency fosters trust. Your peers or people around you see you as being human.
- **Reliability:** People should feel confident that they can rely on you in any situation. This involves being dependable in both small tasks as well as major tasks.

Maintaining Trust:

- **Regular Check-Ins:** Periodically assess your relationships and the level of trust you've built. Address any issues immediately to prevent erosion of trust. This can be in the form of a quick chat with your peers or even walking over to the break room to catch-up.
- **Feedback Loops:** Encourage honest feedback from your team and peers to understand how your actions are perceived. This helps in adjusting your approach to maintain trust.
- **Keep things Professional:** Remember that your personal life and work should not be intertwined. Meaning if you get brutally harsh feedback from your peer, don't take it to heart. Keep it professional and truly look at the feedback.

Emotional Quotient (EQ)

Understanding and Managing Emotions in the Workplace

Emotional Quotient, or EQ, is the ability to understand, use, and manage your emotions in positive ways to communicate effectively, empathize with others, overcome challenges, and defuse conflict. For a Fixer, high EQ is essential because you often work in high-stress environments where emotions can run high.

Components of EQ:

- **Self-Awareness:** Recognizing your own emotional state and understanding how it affects your thoughts and behaviour. This awareness helps you manage your emotions more effectively.
- **Self-Regulation:** The ability to control impulsive

feelings and behaviours, manage your emotions in healthy ways, and take initiative. Figuring out how to self-regulate your emotions in a high-stress situation is vital.

- **Empathy:** Understanding the emotions of others. This allows you to manage relationships more effectively and navigate the social complexities of the workplace.
- **Social Skills:** Building rapport with others to move them in your desired direction. This involves effective communication, active listening, and conflict resolution.

Developing EQ:

- **Practice Active Listening:** Pay full attention to the speaker, avoid interrupting. Take time to understand what is being said before asking questions or responding.
- **Mindfulness:** Regular practice of mindfulness in your daily activities; this will naturally transform your thought process towards being more self-aware and it will teach you to manage your emotions better.
- **Role-Playing Scenarios:** Engage in role-playing exercises to practice empathy and improve your ability to handle emotionally charged situations.

Action

Decisive Action: The Core of a Fixer's Effectiveness

A Fixer is defined by their ability to act, often under pressure and with incomplete information. The capacity to make decisions swiftly and effectively sets you apart in environments where hesitation can lead to missed opportunities or escalated problems.

Key Aspects of Decisive Action:

- **Proactiveness:** Anticipating problems before they arise and taking steps to prevent them. This involves staying informed about trends and potential risks.
- **Risk Management:** Weighing the potential risks and rewards of any action. Having mitigation plans ready and being prepared to pivot if necessary.
- **Implementation:** Execution is critical. A Fixer not only decides on a course of action but also ensures that it is carried out effectively.

Strategies for Effective Action:

- **Prioritize Urgency:** Differentiate between what is urgent and what is important. Address urgent issues immediately but ensure that important tasks are not neglected.
- **Delegate Wisely:** Recognize when to take direct action and when to delegate to others who may be better suited for specific tasks.
- **Learn from Every Action:** After every major decision or action, conduct a post-mortem to understand what worked, what didn't, and why. This continuous learning loop helps refine your decision-making process.
- **Make Decisions Fast:** Being a fixer means that your mind is trained to make decisions quickly by weighing all probable outcomes fast before making the most effective decision. By the time your peers have taken an action you should already made several mistakes and made corrections to your decision. It is alright to make mistakes, but the name of the game is speed for a Fixer.

Logic

Logic and Reasoning: The Anchor of Sound Decision-Making

While emotions and instincts play a role in decision-making, logic ensures that your actions are based on solid reasoning. For a Fixer, applying logic to solve problems and make decisions is crucial to achieving sustainable outcomes.

Elements of Logical Decision-Making:

- **Critical Thinking:** Analysing facts, data, and evidence before making a decision. This involves questioning assumptions, evaluating sources, and considering multiple perspectives.
- **Problem-Solving:** Breaking down complex problems into manageable parts, identifying the root causes, and developing effective solutions.
- **Data-Driven Decisions:** Using data and analytics to inform your decisions. This reduces bias and helps in making more objective choices.

Applying Logic in Real-Life Scenarios:

- **Decision Trees:** Visualize the possible outcomes of different decisions to evaluate the best course of action.
- **Cost-Benefit Analysis:** Assess the potential benefits of an action against the costs involved. This helps in making decisions that maximize positive outcomes while minimizing negative impacts.
- **Effectiveness:** Always make a decision with the largest amount of impact and minimal downside.

The T.E.A.L framework is the cornerstone of being an effective Fixer. By investing time in fully understanding and honing these principles, you're already more than halfway toward becoming an exceptional Fixer. These elements form the foundation of your role, providing you with a distinct and powerful skill set that is rare and highly sought after. Mastering T.E.A.L gives you the tools needed to navigate challenges and deliver impactful results in any situation.

CHAPTER 4: YOUR LEADERSHIP STYLE

Leadership is a multifaceted skill that involves influencing others to achieve a common goal. As a Fixer, understanding and adapting your leadership style to various situations is critical for success. In reality you cannot and should not use one leadership style for everyone. Everyone is unique and so your approach should vary with the people you interact with.

Transformational Leadership

Inspiring Change and Innovation

Transformational leaders inspire and motivate their teams to exceed expectations by creating a compelling vision of the future. They focus on building strong relationships with their team members and are highly effective in environments that require significant change.

Characteristics of Transformational Leaders:

- **Visionary:** They have a clear vision of where they want to take their organisation and can communicate this vision in a way that motivates others.
- **Inspirational Motivation:** They inspire and motivate their team to achieve beyond what they thought possible, often by challenging the status quo.
- **Individualized Consideration:** They recognize the unique needs and strengths of each team member and

provide personalized support to help them grow.

- **Intellectual Stimulation:** They encourage creativity and innovation by challenging assumptions and encouraging new ideas.

When to Use Transformational Leadership:

- **During organisational Change:** When a company is going through significant changes, such as a merger or reorganisation, transformational leadership can help guide the team through uncertainty.
- **To Drive Innovation:** In industries where innovation is key, transformational leaders can inspire their teams to develop new ideas and approaches.

Servant Leadership
Prioritizing the Needs of Others

Servant leaders focus on the growth and well-being of their teams. They prioritize the needs of their employees and believe that when their team members are supported and fulfilled, they will perform at their best.

Key Principles of Servant Leadership:

- **Empathy:** Understanding and sharing the feelings of others. This helps in building strong, trusting relationships with team members.
- **Listening:** Actively listening to understand the concerns and ideas of others.
- **Healing:** Fostering a sense of well-being and helping team members overcome personal and professional challenges.

- **Community Building:** Creating a strong sense of community within the team, where collaboration and mutual support are the norms.

When to Use Servant Leadership:
- **To Improve Team Morale:** In situations where team morale is low, servant leadership can help rebuild trust and create a positive work environment.
- **In Highly Collaborative Environments:** When the success of the team depends on close collaboration, servant leadership can foster the necessary trust and cooperation.

Situational Leadership

Adapting to the Needs of the Moment

Situational leadership involves adapting your leadership style based on the needs of the situation and the maturity of the team. It's about being flexible and choosing the right approach for each scenario.

The Four Leadership Styles in Situational Leadership:
- **Directing:** High direction, low support. Use this style when team members are inexperienced or need clear guidance.
- **Coaching:** High direction, high support. Use this style when team members need both guidance and encouragement.
- **Supporting:** Low direction, high support. Use this style when team members are capable but lack confidence.
- **Delegating:** Low direction, low support. Use this style when team members are experienced and confident,

allowing them to take full responsibility for their tasks.

When to Use Situational Leadership:

- **In Diverse Teams:** When leading a team with varying levels of experience and competence, situational leadership allows you to provide the right level of support to each individual.

- **During Transition Periods:** When team roles or dynamics are changing, situational leadership helps ensure that everyone receives the guidance they need to succeed.

After nearly a decade of working across various industries, I've learned that the ability to adapt my leadership style to fit the situation is critical to success. Truly understanding the people you're working with and recognizing what approach best suits them or the situation at hand gives you an edge as a Fixer. To excel, you need to continuously evolve the way you approach challenges, tailoring your leadership to inspire, support, and guide in a way that transforms outcomes and elevates your impact.

CHAPTER 5: DECENTRALIZED LEARNING THEORY

Decentralized learning recognizes that learning is a continuous, multifaceted process that occurs in various settings beyond formal education. For a Fixer, this approach to learning is essential for staying adaptable and informed in a rapidly changing world.

The Power of Informal Learning

Learning Beyond the Classroom

Informal learning happens outside of a structured curriculum and often occurs through experience, observation, and interaction. As a Fixer, embracing informal learning enables you to acquire knowledge and skills in real-time, adapting quickly to new challenges.

Forms of Informal Learning:

- **On-the-Job Experience:** Learning by doing, where practical experience enhances your understanding of tasks and responsibilities.
- **Collaborative Learning:** Gaining knowledge through interactions with people, whether through direct collaboration or keen observation.
- **Self-Directed Learning:** Taking the initiative to explore topics of interest through reading, online courses, or

experimenting with new tools and techniques.

Maximizing Informal Learning:

- **Stay Curious:** Cultivate a habit of asking questions and seeking out new information, whether through conversations, articles, or experimentation.
- **Reflect on Experiences:** Regularly reflect on your experiences to identify lessons learned and areas for improvement.
- **Seek Feedback:** Actively seek feedback from peers and mentors to gain insights into your performance and areas where you can grow.

Peer-to-Peer Learning

Leveraging Collective Knowledge

For a Fixer, peer-to-peer learning is an essential strategy for harnessing the collective knowledge within a team or organisation. By engaging in this collaborative approach, a Fixer can not only enhance their own skills but also drive the continuous learning and development of those around them.

Implementing Peer-to-Peer Learning:

- **Enhanced Knowledge Sharing:** A Fixer uses peer-to-peer learning to facilitate the exchange of ideas and best practices across the team. By actively engaging with colleagues, the Fixer gains diverse perspectives and insights, which can be crucial when addressing complex challenges.
- **Identifying and Learning from Mentors:** A Fixer strategically identifies experienced individuals within the organisation and learns from them. This targeted

learning allows the Fixer to quickly acquire new skills and knowledge, which can be applied to solving critical issues.

- **Driving Collaborative Projects:** A Fixer leads or participates in projects that require diverse skills and perspectives. By encouraging collaboration, the Fixer not only enhances their own understanding but also creates a culture where innovation and problem-solving thrive. By working closely with others, a Fixer can explore different approaches and uncover innovative solutions that might not emerge in isolation.

- **Facilitating Knowledge Sharing Sessions:** A Fixer organises and leads regular sessions where team members can share insights, tools, and techniques. These sessions are invaluable for spreading knowledge, fostering creativity, and ensuring that the team as a whole is continuously learning and improving.

- **Increased Engagement and Influence:** A Fixer who fosters peer-to-peer learning within the team can enhance engagement and establish themselves as a leader. When team members feel valued for their contributions and see the Fixer as a catalyst for their development, your influence and effectiveness are significantly amplified.

Learning from Failure

Turning Setbacks into Opportunities

Failure is an inevitable part of any career, but it can also be one of the most powerful learning experiences. A Fixer understands that failures provide valuable lessons that can lead to future success.

The Importance of Failure in Learning:

- **Identifying Weaknesses:** Failures often highlight areas where skills, processes, or strategies need improvement.
- **Building Resilience:** Learning to cope with and recover from failure builds mental toughness and adaptability.
- **Encouraging Innovation:** A willingness to fail encourages experimentation and innovation, as team members feel safe taking risks.

Strategies for Learning from Failure:

- **Reflect and Analyse:** After a failure, take time to reflect on what went wrong and why. Analyse the factors that contributed to the outcome and identify what you could do differently next time.
- **Share Lessons Learned:** Discuss failures openly with your team to ensure that everyone can learn from the experience. This also helps create a culture where failure is seen as a learning opportunity rather than something to be feared.
- **Apply Insights:** Use the lessons learned from failures to inform future decisions and strategies, ensuring that past mistakes are not repeated.

Throughout my career, I've relied heavily on decentralized learning, as traditional academic routes never made sense to me. I've always learned by doing, applying the same principles outlined here to become proficient in my field. The depth of understanding gained through this practical, hands-on approach far surpasses what can be obtained in a classroom setting. In today's world, with the explosion of technology and e-learning resources—such as online courses, social media videos, and an abundance of free content—the opportunities for self-directed learning are endless. Take the time to explore various sources, conduct thorough research, and continuously expand your knowledge base. Stay open to new ideas, test them in practice, and ultimately adopt what works best for you.

CHAPTER 6: 0 TO 100

Reaching a flow state, where you're fully immersed in an activity and performing at your peak, is crucial for maximizing productivity and creativity. In this chapter, we'll explore how to achieve and sustain this optimal state. As a Fixer, tapping into flow is not just beneficial, it's essential. Given the complexity and demands of your work, you'll need to enter and maintain this state for extended periods to deliver the high-impact results required of your role.

Understanding Flow

The Psychology of Flow

Flow is a mental state in which a person performing an activity is fully immersed in a feeling of energized focus, full involvement, and enjoyment in the process. This state is often referred to as being "in the zone."

Characteristics of Flow:

- **Complete Concentration:** In a flow state, you are fully focused on the task at hand, with no distractions.
- **Clarity of Goals:** You have a clear understanding of what you need to achieve and how to achieve it.
- **Immediate Feedback:** You receive immediate feedback on your performance, allowing you to adjust your actions as needed.
- **Balance Between Challenge and Skill:** The task at

hand is challenging but achievable, providing a perfect balance between difficulty and your skill level.

Benefits of Flow:

- **Increased Productivity:** Flow allows you to work at your peak performance, completing tasks more efficiently.
- **Enhanced Creativity:** The deep focus of flow often leads to creative breakthroughs and innovative solutions.
- **Improved Well-being:** Achieving flow can lead to greater job satisfaction and a sense of fulfilment.

Techniques to Achieve Flow
Creating the Conditions for Optimal Performance

Achieving flow requires creating the right conditions, both internally and externally. Here are some techniques to help you reach a flow state:

- **Set Clear Goals:** Break down your tasks into specific, achievable and measurable? goals. Having clear objectives provides direction and helps maintain focus.
- **Minimize Distractions:** Create a distraction-free environment by turning off notifications, closing unnecessary tabs, and setting boundaries with colleagues or family members.
- **Match the Challenge to Your Skills:** Ensure that the task is challenging enough to keep you engaged but not so difficult that it becomes frustrating. If a task is too easy, increase the difficulty by setting stricter deadlines or adding complexity.
- **Take Short Breaks:** Regular breaks are essential to maintain focus and prevent burnout. Use techniques like the Pomodoro Technique, where you work for 25

minutes and then take a 5-minute break.
- **Practice Mindfulness:** Mindfulness practices, such as meditation or deep breathing exercises, can help you stay present and focused, making it easier to enter a flow state.

Maintaining Momentum
Sustaining the Flow State Over Time

Once you've achieved flow, maintaining it can be challenging, especially as the initial excitement of a task wanes. Here are some strategies to help you sustain flow:

- **Create a Routine:** Establish a daily routine that supports your flow state. This could include starting your workday with a specific ritual, such as reviewing your goals or engaging in a brief meditation session.
- **Stay Physically Energized:** Physical well-being is closely linked to mental performance. Regular exercise, a healthy diet, and sufficient sleep are crucial for sustaining energy levels throughout the day.
- **Reflect and Adjust:** Periodically reflect on your progress and adjust your approach as needed. If you find yourself slipping out of flow, identify the cause and make changes to regain your focus.
- **Celebrate Small Wins:** Recognize and celebrate your achievements, no matter how small. This positive reinforcement can help maintain motivation and momentum.

Flow state has become one of the most powerful tools in my arsenal. Over the years, I've trained myself to enter it at will and sustain it for extended periods, sometimes for as long as 5 to 6 hours straight. For over 15 years, I've followed a specific routine that primes me for this deep focus. I wake up at 3 a.m., start with a workout that includes weightlifting and some form of cardio—whether it's running, cycling, or intervals—then have breakfast, spend time with my family, prepare meals for the day, and finally settle into work. This ritual sets the stage for me to tap into the flow state and remain productive for hours.

CHAPTER 7: PERCEPTION

Perception, both internal and external, plays a crucial role in shaping your success as a Fixer and the overall trajectory of any organisation you work with. This chapter explores strategies for managing and leveraging perception effectively.

Managing Internal Perception

Influencing how You are Viewed within an Organisation

How you are perceived by your colleagues, superiors, and subordinates can significantly impact your ability to lead, influence decisions, and drive change. As a Fixer, managing internal perception is crucial for building credibility and trust.

Strategies for Managing Internal Perception:

- **Demonstrate Competence:** Consistently deliver high-quality work and demonstrate your expertise in key areas. Competence is the foundation of a positive internal perception.

- **Build Relationships:** Cultivate strong relationships with colleagues at all levels. Building rapport and trust with others enhances your influence and support network.

- **Communicate Effectively:** Be clear, concise, and transparent in your communication. Regularly update stakeholders on your progress and achievements, all while ensuring that your contributions are recognized.

- **Seek Feedback:** Actively seek feedback from colleagues

and superiors to understand how you are perceived and identify areas for improvement. Use this feedback to adjust your approach and enhance your internal image.

External Perception

Managing your Personal and Professional Brand

In today's connected world, your external perception—how you are viewed by clients, industry peers, and the public—can have a significant impact on your career and the success of any organisation you work with. Managing your personal and professional brand is essential for maintaining a positive external image.

Key Elements of External Perception:

- **Online Presence:** Your online presence, including your social media profiles, website, and public statements, plays a significant role in shaping how you are perceived externally. Ensure that your online presence aligns with your professional goals and values.
- **Networking:** Building and maintaining a strong professional network is crucial for managing external perception. Attend industry events, participate in relevant discussions, and contribute to your field to enhance your reputation.
- **Public Relations:** Effective public relations strategies can help you manage your external image. This includes handling media interactions, managing crisis situations, and proactively sharing positive news about your achievements and contributions.

Strategies for Enhancing External Perception:

- **Consistent Branding:** Ensure that all your external communications, from social media posts to public speaking engagements, are consistent with your brand and message.
- **Thought Leadership:** Establish yourself as a thought leader in your industry by sharing insights, publishing articles, and speaking at conferences. This positions you as an expert and enhances your credibility.
- **Community Involvement:** Engage with your community and contribute to causes that align with your values. This not only enhances your external perception but also builds goodwill and strengthens your network.

Open vs. Closed Mindset

Fostering a Culture of Openness and Growth

A Fixer must cultivate an open mindset, always ready to learn, adapt, and grow. In contrast, a closed mindset can limit your potential and hinder your ability to drive change.

Characteristics of an Open Mindset:

- **Willingness to Learn:** An open mindset is characterized by a curiosity and eagerness to learn. This includes being open to new ideas, feedback, and different perspectives.
- **Adaptability:** Those with an open mindset are more adaptable to change. They see challenges as opportunities to grow and are willing to step out of their comfort zones.
- **Collaboration:** An open mindset fosters collaboration, as it values the input and expertise of others. This leads

to more effective teamwork and innovation.

Characteristics of a Closed Mindset:

- **Resistance to Change:** A closed mindset is often resistant to change and prefers to stick with familiar approaches, even when they are no longer effective.
- **Fear of Failure:** Those with a closed mindset often fear failure and avoid taking risks. This can stifle creativity and limit opportunities for growth.
- **Limited Perspective:** A closed mindset can lead to a narrow perspective, where new ideas and feedback are dismissed, leading to missed opportunities.

Strategies for Fostering an Open Mindset:

- **Encourage Continuous Learning:** Promote a culture of learning and development within your team. Provide opportunities for professional growth, such as training programs, workshops, and mentorship.
- **Embrace Failure:** Create an environment where failure is seen as a learning opportunity rather than a setback. Encourage team members to take risks and experiment with new ideas.
- **Promote Diversity of Thought:** Encourage diverse perspectives and ideas within your team. This can lead to more innovative solutions and a more dynamic work environment.
- **Lead by Example:** As a Fixer, demonstrate an open mindset in your own actions. Show that you value learning, adaptability, and collaboration, and your team will be more likely to adopt these behaviours.

Every interaction you have shapes how others perceive you. From the first moment, people evaluate your appearance, demeanour, and how you communicate. This is an instinctual process, deeply ingrained in human nature. As a Fixer, it's vital to recognize that both perception and mindset are critical to your effectiveness. The way others see you will influence how they trust and engage with you. Your most important asset is people and projecting your values clearly while maintaining an open mindset helps to foster trust and credibility. By managing perception wisely, you lay the foundation for strong relationships that elevate your personal and professional growth.

CHAPTER 8: THE BIG PICTURE

Understanding the broader context of your work and aligning your efforts with the organisation's strategic goals is crucial for long-term success. This chapter explores how to think strategically and contribute to the overall mission and vision of the organisation.

Strategic Vision

Aligning Your Efforts with the organisation's Goals

A Fixer must always keep the big picture in mind, ensuring that their actions align with the organisation's strategic vision. This involves understanding the company's long-term goals and how your work contributes to achieving them.

Key Elements of Strategic Vision:

- **Mission and Vision Statement:** Understand the organisation's mission and vision statements, which defines its purpose and core values.
- **Long-Term Goals:** Familiarize yourself with the organisation's long-term goals and objectives, which provide direction for its growth and development.
- **Market Positioning and Value Proposition:** Understand where the organisation stands in the market and how it differentiates itself from competitors.

Contributing to the Strategic Vision:

- **Align Your Goals:** Ensure that your personal and team goals align with the organisation's strategic vision. This helps in prioritizing tasks that have the most significant impact on the company's success.

- **Communicate the Vision:** Regularly communicate the strategic vision to your team to ensure that everyone is working towards the same objectives.

- **Stay Informed:** Keep yourself informed about changes in the industry, market trends, and the competitive landscape. This allows you to adjust your strategies to stay aligned with the organisation's goals.

Balancing Short-Term Wins with Long-Term Goals

Maintaining Focus on Both Immediate and Future Success

While short-term wins are essential for maintaining momentum and motivation, a Fixer must also ensure that these achievements contribute to long-term success.

Strategies for Balancing Short-Term and Long-Term Focus:

- **Prioritize High-Impact Tasks:** Focus on tasks that have both immediate benefits and contribute to long-term goals.

- **Avoid Short-Term Fixes:** Be cautious of solutions that provide short-term relief but may create long-term problems. Always consider the long-term implications of your actions.

- **Celebrate Successes:** Recognize achievements of your peers and celebrate short-term wins, but always keep the bigger picture in mind. Use these successes as stepping stones towards achieving long-term goals.

Long-Term Planning

Balancing Immediate Needs with Future Goals

While it's essential to focus on day-to-day tasks, a Fixer must also keep an eye on the future. Long-term planning involves setting milestones and developing strategies that ensure sustained success.

Elements of Long-Term Planning:

- **Setting Milestones:** Break down long-term goals into smaller, manageable milestones. This helps in tracking progress and staying on course.

- **Resource Allocation:** Ensure that resources, such as time, budget, and personnel, are allocated effectively to achieve long-term goals.

- **Risk Management:** Identify potential risks that could impact long-term success and develop contingency plans to mitigate them.

Implementing Long-Term Planning:

- **Strategic Roadmaps:** Create a strategic roadmap that outlines the steps needed to achieve long-term goals. This should include timelines, resource allocation, and key milestones.

- **Regular Review:** Periodically review your progress towards long-term goals and adjust your plans as needed, to stay on track.

- **Engage Stakeholders:** Involve key stakeholders in the planning process to ensure that everyone is aligned and committed to achieving the long-term vision.

As a Fixer, you'll often find yourself navigating situations where people are not aligned with the organisation's goal. In these instances, it's essential to first gain clarity from the management team and identify the root causes of these disconnects. Misalignments typically arise from poor communication, unestablished processes, or conflicting priorities around deliverables. To be most effective, consider using visual tools like mind maps, or vision boards (e.g. Miro, Figma, Microsoft Visio). These tools help you visualize the big picture, map out key milestones, and define both short- and long-term goals. Since people are inherently visual, providing a clear picture of the end goal is often more impactful than verbal explanations alone, allowing teams to align more easily and drive forward with a shared vision.

CHAPTER 9: BLUEPRINTS TO SCALE

Scaling a business involves more than just growing its size; it requires strategic planning, execution, and the ability to navigate challenges. This chapter explores the essential tools and strategies for successfully scaling an organisation.

SWOT Analysis in Practice

Leveraging Strengths, Weaknesses, Opportunities, and Threats

A SWOT analysis is a tried and tested powerful tool that helps you assess the organisation's internal strengths and weaknesses, as well as external opportunities and threats. This analysis is critical for developing a strategy to scale a business effectively.

Steps to Conduct a SWOT Analysis:

- **Identify Strengths:** Assess the organisation's internal strengths, such as a strong brand, loyal customer base, or unique technology. Leverage these strengths to capitalize on opportunities.
- **Acknowledge Weaknesses:** Identify internal weaknesses, such as limited resources, skills gaps, or operational inefficiencies. Develop strategies to address these weaknesses, ideally with the goal to reduce its overall impact.
- **Explore Opportunities:** Look for external opportunities that align with the organisation's strengths, such as new

markets, emerging technologies, or changing consumer trends.

- **Mitigate Threats:** Identify potential external threats, such as new competitors, regulatory changes, or economic downturns. Develop contingency plans to mitigate these risks.

Using SWOT to Inform Scaling Strategies:

- **Prioritize Opportunities:** Focus on opportunities that align with the organisation's strengths and offer the greatest potential for growth.

- **Address Weaknesses:** Develop action plans to strengthen the organisation's weaknesses, ensuring that they do not hinder the ability to scale.

- **Prepare for Threats:** Proactively address potential threats by developing strategies to mitigate their impact on the business.

Identifying the Right Audience

Targeting the Demographics That Matter

Understanding and targeting the right audience is critical for successful scaling. Without a clear understanding of who the organisation's customers are, efforts to scale may be inefficient or ineffective.

Steps to Identify the Target Audience:

- **Market Segmentation:** Divide the broader market into smaller segments based on demographics, psychographics, behaviour, and geography. This helps you identify the specific groups most likely to benefit from the organisation's products or services.

- **Customer Persona Development:** Create detailed customer personas that represent the organisation's ideal customers. These personas should include information about their needs, preferences, pain points, and buying behaviour.
- **Analyse Competitor Audiences:** Study the target audiences of the competitors. Understanding who they are targeting can provide insights into potential gaps in the market that the organisation can exploit.

Strategies to Target the Right Audience:

- **Tailored Marketing:** Develop marketing campaigns that speak directly to the needs and desires of the organisation's target audience. Use language, imagery, and channels that resonate with them.
- **Product Customisation:** Customise the organisation's products or services to meet the specific needs of your target audience. This could involve developing new features, offering different pricing tiers, or providing personalized experiences.
- **Feedback Loops:** Continuously gather feedback from the target audience to refine your approach. Use surveys, focus groups, and social media listening to stay in tune with their evolving needs.

The Messy Middle

Navigating the Complexities of Scaling

Scaling is rarely a straightforward process. The Messy Middle refers to the unpredictable and often challenging period between a business's early successes and its eventual establishment as a dominant player in its market. This concept was described in detail in the book 'The Messy Middle by Scott Belsky'.

Challenges of the Messy Middle:

- **Resource Constraints:** As the organisation grows, you may encounter resource constraints, such as limited capital, personnel, or infrastructure.
- **Operational Complexity:** Scaling often introduces new operational complexities, such as managing larger teams, maintaining quality control, and ensuring consistent customer experiences.
- **Market Saturation:** As the organisation scales, you may face increased competition and market saturation, making it harder to maintain growth.

Strategies for Navigating the Messy Middle:

- **Flexible Planning:** Develop flexible strategies that allow you to pivot quickly in response to new challenges or opportunities. This involves regularly reviewing and adjusting your plans as needed.
- **Focus on Core Strengths:** During periods of rapid growth, it's easy to get distracted by new opportunities. Stay focused on your core strengths and ensure that they remain at the heart of your business strategy.
- **Build Resilience:** Prepare for setbacks by building resilience into the organisation. This could involve diversifying revenue streams, maintaining a healthy cash reserve, and fostering a culture of adaptability.

Scaling a business is often one of the most intricate challenges a Fixer faces. It requires a deep understanding of the organisation's inner workings—its operations, limitations, and competitive landscape. As a Fixer, it's crucial to dedicate time to thoroughly analyse the business, identify gaps, and develop strategies that prioritize efficiency and impact. Remember, no organisation has infinite resources, so every recommendation you put forward must deliver maximum results with minimal time to implement and begin generating returns. Scaling is not a rapid process; it demands both strategic planning and patience. Trust the process and stay committed for the long haul.

CHAPTER 10: PRECIOUS RESOURCE

People are the lifeblood of any organisation, and as a Fixer, their well-being, development, and engagement are vital to achieving long-term success. Your ability to drive meaningful results depends on the strength of your team and how well they collaborate with you. It's not just about getting things done—it's about genuinely caring for the people around you and fostering strong, productive relationships. When you invest in your team, you're not only supporting their growth but also ensuring that they are fully aligned and engaged in helping you succeed as a Fixer.

Employee Well-being

The Link Between Well-being and Productivity

Employee well-being encompasses physical, mental, and emotional health. A healthy and happy workforce is more engaged, productive, and loyal. For a Fixer, promoting well-being is not just about being compassionate; it's a strategic move to enhance overall performance.

Components of Employee Well-being:

- **Physical Health:** Providing resources and initiatives that promote physical health, such as fitness programs, healthy food options, and ergonomic workspaces.
- **Mental Health:** Offering mental health support,

including counselling services, stress management programs, professional coaching services and promoting work-life balance.
- **Work-Life Balance:** Encouraging flexible work arrangements and ensuring that employees have time to recharge and maintain a healthy work-life balance.

Strategies to Enhance Well-being:
- **Wellness Programs:** Implement comprehensive wellness programs that address physical, mental, and emotional health. This could include gym memberships, meditation sessions, and access to mental health resources.
- **Supportive Work Environment:** Create a work environment that encourages open communication, provides support for stress management, and recognizes the importance of work-life balance.
- **Regular Check-Ins:** Conduct regular check-ins with employees to assess their well-being and address any concerns they may have. This helps in identifying potential issues before they escalate.

Talent Development
Nurturing and Growing Your Team's Potential
Developing the skills and talents of your team is essential for both individual and organisational growth. A Fixer must focus on creating opportunities for continuous learning and development.

Key Aspects of Talent Development:
- **Continuous Learning:** Encourage a culture of continuous learning by providing access to training

programs, workshops, and other educational resources.

- **Career Growth Opportunities:** Create clear pathways for career advancement within the organisation, ensuring that employees see a future with the company.
- **Mentorship and Coaching:** Pair employees with mentors or coaches who can guide their development and help them achieve their career goals.

Implementing Talent Development Strategies:

- **Personalized Development Plans:** Work with each employee to create a personalized development plan that aligns with their career aspirations and the needs of the organisation.
- **Learning and Development Programs:** Invest in learning and development programs that provide employees with the skills and knowledge they need to succeed in their roles and advance in their careers.
- **Recognition and Reward:** Recognize and reward employees for their efforts in developing new skills and taking on additional responsibilities. This motivates them to continue growing.

Retention Strategies

Keeping Your Top Talent Engaged and Committed

Retaining top talent is a significant challenge for many organisations. A Fixer needs to develop strategies that keep employees engaged, motivated, and loyal to the company.

Factors Influencing Retention:

- **Job Satisfaction:** Ensuring that employees find their work meaningful, and fulfilling is key to retention. This includes providing challenging work, opportunities for growth, and recognition for their contributions.

- **Compensation and Benefits:** Competitive salaries and benefits packages are essential for retaining top talent. However, non-monetary benefits, such as flexible work arrangements and professional development opportunities, are also important.
- **Work Environment:** A positive work environment where employees feel valued and respected is crucial for retention. This includes fostering a culture of inclusion, respect, and collaboration.

Strategies to Improve Retention:

- **Engagement Surveys:** Conduct regular employee engagement surveys to understand what motivates your team and what areas need improvement. Use the feedback to make necessary changes.
- **Career Development:** Provide clear pathways for career advancement and opportunities for employees to take on new challenges and responsibilities.
- **Recognition Programs:** Implement recognition programs that celebrate employees' achievements and contributions, reinforcing their value to the organisation.

In my recent organisation, I applied these principles by leveraging my past experience to demonstrate my expertise. Drawing on the skills I developed in previous roles, I earned the management team's trust to lead initiatives that involved conducting thorough analyses, gathering key insights, and determining the best strategies for scaling the business. Some of the proposals I introduced included implementing company-sponsored medical insurance, establishing structured performance reviews with clear grading systems to identify top performers, and offering promotions or salary increases where appropriate. Additionally, I recommended providing optional access to professional coaching, with one-on-one coaching for the leadership team to help them enhance their leadership skills and ensure they were fostering an environment that retained talent and supported organisational growth.

CHAPTER 11: NAVIGATING DIGITAL TRANSFORMATION

In today's business world, technological disruption is constant, and a Fixer must be well-versed in navigating digital transformation. Whether it's implementing new tools, optimizing workflows with automation, or adapting to the rise of AI, the ability to understand and lead through these changes is critical.

Digital Transformation

Digital transformation is more than just adopting the latest technology; it's about leveraging technology to drive growth, improve efficiency, and deliver better customer experiences. As a Fixer, you need to ensure that these innovations align with the organisation's strategic goals and don't become distractions.

Steps for Leading Digital Transformation:

- **Identify Opportunities for Automation:** Start by assessing areas where automation can save time and increase efficiency. Whether through AI-driven customer support or automated data processing, these tools allow you to shift focus to higher-level strategic tasks.

- **Invest in Data Analytics:** Make informed decisions by leveraging data analytics. Understanding the organisation's data can provide critical insights into customer behaviour, operational efficiency, and future trends.

- **Bridge the Digital Skill Gap:** As technology evolves, the skillsets of your team must evolve too. Offer training and development opportunities to ensure your team can effectively use new tools and technologies.
- **Leading Change:** Digital transformation often triggers resistance from teams, so a Fixer must lead by example. Communicate the benefits of change clearly and consistently, addressing concerns and showing the team how the new tools will make their jobs easier.

To successfully drive digital transformation, staying informed about the latest trends in operational improvements is essential. This can be as simple as subscribing to newsletters from reputable sources like Tech Brew or The AI Break or setting up Google Alerts for keywords that align with the organisation's digital focus. As a Fixer, your role is to identify how emerging technologies can streamline processes, replace manual tasks, and enhance efficiency. Understanding what tools are available, and how they can be leveraged to optimize operations will be crucial in your mission to guide organisations through digital transformation.

CHAPTER 12: INCLUSIVE LEADERSHIP AND THE POWER OF DIVERSITY

In today's workforce, diversity is not just a buzzword; it's a crucial element of success. As a Fixer, it's essential to lead with inclusivity, ensuring that diverse perspectives are valued and contribute to better problem-solving and innovation.

Understanding Inclusive Leadership

Inclusive leadership is about creating a culture where every team member feels valued, respected, and empowered to contribute their unique perspective. This means actively seeking out diverse voices and recognizing that inclusivity leads to better decision-making and stronger outcomes.

Key Elements of Inclusive Leadership:

- **Fostering Psychological Safety:** Create an environment where team members feel safe to express their ideas without fear of judgment.
- **Embracing Cultural Competence:** Understand and respect the diverse cultural backgrounds of your team members and be sensitive to their individual needs.
- **Encouraging Diverse Perspectives:** Actively invite different viewpoints into discussions. This diversity of thought often leads to more creative and innovative

solutions.

Actionable Steps for a Fixer:

- **Build a Diverse Team:** Ensure your hiring practices focus on diversity and inclusion. Diverse teams are shown to be more innovative and effective.
- **Lead with Empathy:** As a Fixer, emotional intelligence is key. Listen actively and demonstrate empathy toward your team members to foster stronger connections and trust.
- **Leverage Diversity for Innovation:** When you embrace different viewpoints, you open the door for new ways of solving problems—one of the Fixer's core missions.

No one can know everything, and as a Fixer, this is a principle you must live by. Every individual, regardless of age, gender, or experience, has valuable insights, and it's your responsibility to ensure their voices are heard. Your role as a Fixer is to weigh these diverse perspectives, analyse them critically, and determine which ideas can be adopted or adapted to move a project forward, solve a problem, or improve existing practices. By fostering inclusivity and leveraging the collective intelligence of your team, you create a stronger foundation for innovation and progress.

CHAPTER 13: LEADING IN REMOTE AND HYBRID WORK ENVIRONMENTS

The rise of remote and hybrid work has fundamentally changed how we lead teams. As a Fixer, your role in managing distributed teams is vital for maintaining productivity and engagement, regardless of physical distance.

Challenges in Remote Leadership

Remote work introduces unique challenges, including communication barriers, decreased team cohesion, and potential misalignment on goals. A Fixer must overcome these challenges by maintaining strong leadership even from afar.

Strategies for Remote Leadership:

- **Foster Open Communication:** Use digital collaboration tools like Slack, Microsoft Teams, and Zoom to ensure seamless communication. Encourage transparency and frequent check-ins.
- **Define Clear Goals:** In remote environments, clarity becomes even more important. Ensure that all team members understand their responsibilities and deadlines.
- **Cultivate a Virtual Culture:** Don't let physical distance erode your company's culture. Organize virtual team-

building activities and celebrate wins together to foster a sense of belonging.

- **Empowering Your Team:** Remote work requires a high level of trust. Empower your team members by giving them the autonomy to manage their own time and projects while providing the support they need to succeed.

Hybrid teams are undoubtedly here to stay, but one of the significant challenges of remote work is the loss of human connection. As a Fixer, it's essential to address this issue as more organisations shift towards hybrid models instead of returning to full-time office work. The key is to foster regular communication and ensure that every team member feels seen and valued. Frequent check-ins, both formal and informal, will help maintain a sense of belonging and alignment. During the Covid-19 pandemic, many companies successfully used virtual team gatherings, games, and other bonding activities to keep morale high and maintain team cohesion. These are valuable practices you can adopt or refine to create a strong, connected hybrid team, even from a distance.

CHAPTER 14: MANAGING MENTAL HEALTH AND WELL-BEING

In high-pressure roles, maintaining mental health and well-being is critical. As a Fixer, you are not only responsible for your well-being but also for fostering an environment where your team feels supported and valued.

The Importance of Mental Health

When employees feel overwhelmed or burned out, productivity and creativity suffer. By prioritizing mental health, you ensure your team is engaged, motivated, and capable of delivering high-quality work.

Strategies for Promoting Well-Being:

- **Encourage Work-Life Balance:** Promote flexible work arrangements that allow your team to recharge. This could mean offering remote work options, flexible hours, or mental health days.
- **Offer Mental Health Resources:** Provide access to counselling services and wellness programs.
- **Foster Open Communication:** Create an environment where team members feel comfortable discussing their mental health without fear of stigma. Regularly check in with your team to assess their well-being.

- **Respect Individual Boundaries:** Recognise that everyone has their own lives, challenges, and personal situations. Treat others with empathy and respect, honouring their boundaries and supporting their need for balance.

Your ability to manage your own stress and maintain balance directly influences the energy and productivity of your team. As a Fixer, leading by example is essential, and that starts with prioritizing your own well-being. Demonstrating a commitment to self-care not only preserves your effectiveness but also sets a standard for your team. When they see you managing stress, taking breaks when needed, and balancing your workload, it creates a culture where personal well-being is valued. Encourage your team to do the same by creating an open environment where they feel comfortable discussing their challenges and seeking support when needed. Simple practices like encouraging regular breaks, promoting healthy work-life boundaries, and offering resources for mental health can make a significant difference. By modelling this behaviour, you empower your team to perform at their best without sacrificing their mental or physical well-being—building resilience not only for themselves but for the entire organisation.

CHAPTER 15: SUSTAINABILITY AND ETHICAL LEADERSHIP

Sustainability and ethical leadership are no longer optional, they are essential to business success. As a Fixer, your role involves ensuring that every decision you make aligns with both environmental responsibility and ethical principles, all while maintaining profitability.

The Importance of Sustainability

Consumers and employees alike are demanding more from businesses in terms of sustainability. This means integrating eco-friendly practices, reducing waste, and considering the long-term impact of and organisation's decisions.

Key Elements of Sustainability:

- **Eco-Friendly Practices:** Implement processes that reduce waste, conserve energy, and minimize carbon footprints across all operations.
- **Sustainable Supply Chains:** Focus on sourcing materials responsibly, choosing suppliers who consciously prioritise environmental standards and ethical labour practices.
- **Long-Term Environmental Impact:** Evaluate every decision based on its long-term effect on the

environment, ensuring that sustainability is a core part of the organisation's overall strategy.

Incorporating Sustainability as a Fixer:

- **Embed Sustainability into Strategy:** Ensure that every initiative and project considers its environmental impact, integrating sustainability into the organisation's core operations.
- **Promote Green Innovation:** Encourage the development of eco-friendly products, technologies, or solutions that align with the company's sustainability goals.
- **Educate and Empower:** Advocate for sustainability education within the organisation, equipping your team with the knowledge and tools to drive environmentally conscious decisions.

Ethical Leadership

Ethical leadership goes beyond sustainability, it is about fostering an environment where transparency, responsibility, and long-term thinking guide every decision.

Elements of Ethical Leadership:

- **Transparency:** Build trust with stakeholders by being transparent about your decisions, policies, and business practices. Transparent communication with stakeholders is key to fostering long-term relationships.
- **Social Responsibility:** Take responsibility for the social impact of the organisation. This could mean giving back to local communities, advocating for fair labour practices, or initiatives to reduce the organisation's

carbon footprint.

- **Long-Term Thinking:** Ethical leadership requires thinking beyond short-term profits. A Fixer ensures that every decision made today supports long-term sustainability and ethical standards.

Driving Ethical Leadership as a Fixer:

- **Lead by Example:** Model ethical behaviour in all your interactions and decisions. This sets the standard for the rest of the organisation.

- **Incorporate Sustainability into Your Strategy:** Ensure that your projects and initiatives consider their environmental and social impact.

- **Foster a Culture of Integrity:** Cultivate an organisational culture where ethics and integrity are non-negotiable. Empower your team to speak up and address unethical behaviour when it arises.

Sustainability is no longer just a matter of environmental responsibility; it is also what consumers increasingly demand from businesses. The long-term impact organisations have on the planet is significant, and as a Fixer, it is crucial to ensure that sustainability is integrated into your strategic decisions. This means placing sustainability at the forefront of your initiatives, not as an afterthought but as a core consideration in every project. Ethical leadership plays a pivotal role here. Leaders who prioritise ethical decision-making are the ones driving real change, ensuring that business growth goes hand in hand with sustainability.

CHAPTER 16: AGILE LEADERSHIP AND ADAPTABILITY

Agile leadership is a natural extension of the Fixer mentality, emphasizing flexibility, rapid iteration, and a constant feedback loop. In a fast-paced business world where conditions can change in an instant, the ability to adapt quickly and decisively is essential. Agile leadership encourages leaders to respond to new information, adjust their strategies in real-time, and continuously drive projects forward—all qualities that align perfectly with the Fixer's core attributes.

The Agile Approach

Agile leadership is grounded in responsiveness rather than rigid, long-term planning. Unlike traditional methods, which often rely on fixed timelines and detailed step-by-step roadmaps, agile leaders understand that today's dynamic environment demands a more fluid approach. They recognize that change is inevitable, and that success lies in the ability to pivot quickly without losing sight of the larger objectives.

Key Principles of Agile Leadership

- **Iterative Process:** At the heart of agile leadership is the iterative process—breaking projects into manageable tasks that can be completed, assessed, and refined on a continuous basis. This approach allows a Fixer to maintain forward momentum while making real-time adjustments based on new data or circumstances. It also ensures that long-term goals remain aligned with day-to-day progress, without being derailed by unforeseen changes.

- **Feedback Loops:** Agile leadership thrives on open communication and consistent feedback. Fixers must foster an environment where team members feel comfortable sharing insights, concerns, and suggestions. Regular feedback loops prevent minor issues from escalating into major roadblocks and ensure that everyone stays focused on the shared goal. It's about creating a culture where adjustments are made swiftly, not when problems have already snowballed.

- **Cross-Functional Collaboration:** One of the cornerstones of agile leadership is cross-functional collaboration. Fixers are often required to work across multiple departments or disciplines, and agile leadership helps bridge those gaps. By bringing together diverse teams and encouraging open collaboration, Fixers can harness a wide range of perspectives and skills, ultimately driving more innovative solutions and more cohesive teamwork.

Adapting as a Fixer

Adaptability is the cornerstone of both the agile mindset and the Fixer's approach. In an agile environment, setbacks and roadblocks are not viewed as failures but as opportunities to learn and refine strategies. Agile leaders must constantly iterate —not just in their projects, but in their leadership style as well. *(Refer to Chapter 4: Your Leadership Style to recap on the various leadership styles a Fixer should have in their arsenal.)* For a Fixer, this means embracing change and applying lessons learned from each iteration to enhance their decision-making process and execution.

Agility doesn't just apply to project management; it permeates every aspect of leadership, from decision-making to team dynamics. As a Fixer, you must stay attuned to changes in the market, industry trends, and even shifts in team morale. In doing so, you ensure that both your leadership style and your strategies remain relevant, effective, and aligned with the organisation's evolving needs.

Consider a scenario where a company's market shifts unexpectedly due to a new competitor or a technological breakthrough. What would a Fixer do? A Fixer would gather their cross-functional team, assess the new landscape, and quickly redefine their approach. Whether that means reprioritizing deliverables or exploring innovative solutions, the Fixer remains focused on moving forward and delivering value, no matter how the situation changes.

CHAPTER 17: BLUEPRINTS TO START

Starting a new initiative or business requires careful planning and a clear understanding of the steps needed to bring a vision to life. This chapter provides a comprehensive guide to getting started.

Ideation and Validation

From Concept to Reality

Every successful venture begins with a great idea. However, not all ideas are viable, so it's crucial to validate the concept before investing significant time and resources.

Steps in the Ideation Process:

- **Brainstorming:** Generate a wide range of ideas without judgment. Use brainstorming techniques such as mind mapping, free writing, whiteboarding or group sessions to explore different possibilities.
- **Idea Screening:** Evaluate ideas based on criteria such as feasibility, market potential, and alignment with the goals. Narrow down your list to the most promising concepts.
- **Prototyping:** Create a prototype or a minimum viable product (MVP) to test the idea in the real world. This allows you to gather feedback and make necessary adjustments before fully launching.

Validating Your Idea:
- **Market Research:** Conduct thorough market research to assess demand, understand the target demographic, and identify potential competitors. This research helps you validate that there is a need for the product or service.
- **Customer Feedback:** Seek feedback from potential customers through surveys, focus groups, or beta testing. Use this feedback to refine the idea and ensure it meets the needs of the target audience.
- **Financial Viability:** Assess the financial viability of the idea by estimating costs, potential revenue, and profitability. Ensure that the venture is economically sustainable.

Creating a Business Plan
Mapping Out Your Road to Success

A well-structured business plan is essential for guiding a new venture from concept to reality. It serves as a roadmap that outlines the strategy, operational plan, and financial projections.

Key Components of a Business Plan:
- **Executive Summary:** A brief overview of the business, the problem you are trying to solve, the mission and vision statement, product or service offerings, target market, and financial goals.
- **Market Analysis:** An in-depth analysis of the industry, market size, target demographic, and competitive landscape.
- **Marketing and Sales Strategy:** A detailed plan for how customers will be attracted and retained, including

pricing strategy, sales tactics, and promotional activities.
- **Operations Plan:** A description of operational processes, including production, supply chain management, and day-to-day business activities.
- **Financial Plan:** Detailed financial projections, including income statements, cash flow statements, and balance sheets. This section should also include a break-even analysis, funding requirements and funding avenues.

Using Your Business Plan:

- **Guiding Decision-Making:** Use the business plan as a reference point when making strategic decisions, ensuring that your actions align with long-term goals.
- **Attracting Investors:** A comprehensive business plan is essential for attracting investors or securing financing. It demonstrates that you have a clear strategy and a viable path to profitability.
- **Tracking Progress:** Regularly review and update the business plan to reflect changes in the market or the business. This helps stay on track and make informed adjustments as needed.

Building a Core Team

Assembling the Right People for Success

No Fixer can do it alone. Building a core team that shares your vision and complements your skills is critical to the success of starting any venture.

Key Roles in a Core Team:

- **Co-Founder(s):** A co-founder should not only share the

organisation's vision but also bring a skill set that complements and balances your own. This partnership is crucial for driving the business forward and making key strategic decisions. Their expertise should fill the gaps where your own strengths may not lie, creating a dynamic where your weaknesses are supported, not duplicated. In this way, the co-founder amplifies the overall capabilities of the leadership team, allowing the business to thrive through a well-rounded approach to problem-solving and execution.

- **Marketing and Sales Lead:** This role focuses on shaping and executing strategies that drive customer acquisition and retention, ultimately fuelling revenue growth. This individual must cover key areas such as generating innovative ideas, creating compelling content, and leveraging social media marketing to amplify the organisation's reach.
- **Finance Manager:** Responsible for overseeing financial planning, budgeting, and cash flow management, this role ensures the organisation remains financially stable. This individual plays a critical role in balancing remuneration and operational expenses, all while strategically managing resources to support long-term growth and sustainability.

Building a Strong Team Culture:

- **Shared Vision and Values:** Ensure that all team members are aligned with the business' vision and values. This alignment fosters collaboration and a sense of shared purpose.
- **Effective Communication:** Clear and open communication channels are essential to ensure

everyone remains aligned and focused on shared goals. Regular stand-ups, weekly company-wide updates, and consistent feedback loops are crucial practices to keep communication flowing.

- **Continuous Learning:** Encourage a culture of continuous learning and development, where team members are empowered to grow their skills and contribute to the business's success.

Starting is often the most challenging step. As a Fixer, your role is to push past inertia, initiate momentum, and navigate the uncertainties that lie ahead. The unknown is where your creativity will be put to the test, and concepts can be validated through action. Embrace the possibility of failure but focus on fast iterations and continuous improvement. Each step forward offers an opportunity to refine your approach, turning potential setbacks into valuable learning experiences, and ensuring progress in even the most unpredictable situations.

CHAPTER 18: BECOMING THE ULTIMATE FIXER

Bringing It All Together

In this final chapter, we synthesize the concepts, strategies, and tools discussed throughout the book to outline the path to becoming the Ultimate Fixer.

The Fixer Toolkit

Your Comprehensive Guide to Fixing

Throughout this book, we've explored various tools, skills, and frameworks that are essential for a Fixer. In this section, we'll compile them into a comprehensive toolkit that you can refer to as you continue your journey.

Key Components of the Fixer Toolkit:

- **TEAL Framework:** Trust, Emotional Quotient, Action, Logic—these core principles guide every decision and action.
- **Leadership Styles:** Understanding and adapting your leadership style to different situations is critical for driving change and managing teams effectively.
- **Decentralized Learning:** Embrace continuous learning from a variety of sources, encourage peer-to-peer learning and knowledge sharing within your team.
- **Employee Well-being and Talent Development:**

Recognize that people are your most valuable resource. Invest in their well-being, development, and retention to build a strong, motivated team.

- **Strategic Vision and Planning:** Align your efforts with the organisation's strategic goals, balance short-term wins with long-term success, and navigate the complexities of scaling with confidence.

- **Perception Management:** Manage both internal and external perceptions to build credibility, influence, and a positive reputation.

Case Studies and Real-World Applications

Learning from Successful Fixers

To truly understand the power and impact of a Fixer, it's helpful to look at real-world examples of individuals who have demonstrated these principles in action. These case studies showcase how Fixers can navigate complex challenges, transform organisations, and lead with purpose.

Case Study 1: Ed Catmull – The Visionary Fixer at Pixar

- **Background:** In the early 90s, Pixar was a small company with groundbreaking ideas but struggling financially. They were on the cusp of creating the world's first entirely computer-animated movie, but internal challenges and external market scepticism threatened their success.

- **Challenge:** Pixar needed to convince Hollywood of the viability of computer-generated animation, while simultaneously managing internal creative and technical teams through uncharted territory.

- **The Fixer's Approach:** As the co-founder and then-president of Pixar, **Ed Catmull** stepped into the role of a Fixer by fostering a culture of creativity and innovation. He recognized the need to balance the artistic vision with business realities, creating an environment where experimentation was encouraged but aligned with the company's goals. Catmull also broke down silos, ensuring that creative, technical, and management teams collaborated effectively.

- **Outcome:** Under Catmull's leadership, Pixar released *Toy Story* in 1995, revolutionizing the animation industry and establishing Pixar as a powerhouse in the field. His ability to align diverse teams, manage complex challenges, and push the boundaries of technology and storytelling are textbook examples of how a Fixer operates in a high-stakes environment.

Case Study 2: Sheryl Sandberg – The Strategic Fixer at Facebook

- **Background:** When **Sheryl Sandberg** joined Facebook in 2008, the company was popular but far from profitable. It was rapidly scaling, but without a clear path to turning its user base into sustainable revenue.
- **Challenge:** Sandberg was tasked with transforming Facebook's business model and building the operational structures to support its rapid growth, all while maintaining its startup culture.
- **The Fixer's Approach:** Sandberg's strategy was to bring discipline to Facebook's operations. She introduced formal processes for scaling the company's advertising business, created new revenue streams, and implemented a more structured approach to leadership without stifling innovation. Her work as a Fixer focused on operational clarity, team alignment, and

monetization strategies that didn't compromise the user experience.

- **Outcome:** Sandberg's efforts transformed Facebook into one of the most profitable companies in the world, with advertising as its primary revenue engine. Her ability to fix operational inefficiencies while guiding strategic business decisions made her an indispensable part of Facebook's growth.

Case Study 3: Alan Mulally – The Turnaround Fixer at Ford

- **Background:** In 2006, Ford was in dire financial straits, losing billions of dollars and struggling to stay competitive in the automotive industry.
- **Challenge:** Ford needed a complete overhaul of its operations, culture, and product strategy to avoid bankruptcy and regain its market position.
- **The Fixer's Approach: Alan Mulally**, brought in as CEO, immediately set out to transform the company. He introduced a culture of transparency and accountability, focusing on collaboration across all levels of the organisation. Mulally implemented the "One Ford" strategy, which unified global operations and streamlined product development, ensuring that Ford operated as a cohesive, focused entity.
- **Outcome:** Mulally's leadership turned Ford around without government bailout assistance. Under his guidance, Ford returned to profitability, regaining its standing in the industry and positioning itself as a forward-thinking automaker.

Each of these Fixers demonstrates the core principles discussed throughout this book: adaptability, strategic vision, operational clarity, and the ability to align teams around a common purpose. Whether fostering innovation, transforming operational models, or leading a company through a financial turnaround, the impact of these individuals showcases the real-world power of a Fixer.

Your Next Steps

Taking Action and Applying What You've Learned

Now that you've learned the principles and strategies of a Fixer, it's time to take action. The following steps will help you get started.

Steps to Becoming a Fixer:

- **Self-Assessment:** Reflect on your current skills, strengths, and areas for improvement. Identify where you can apply the principles of a Fixer in your work.
- **Set Goals:** Establish clear, actionable goals for developing your skills as a Fixer. This could include improving your leadership style, enhancing your emotional intelligence, or learning new strategic planning techniques.
- **Start Small:** Begin by applying Fixer principles to smaller projects or challenges. As you gain confidence and experience, take on more complex initiatives.
- **Build Your Network:** Surround yourself with other Fixers—people who challenge you, support your growth, and share your vision. This network will be invaluable as you continue your journey.
- **Commit to Continuous Learning:** The journey to becoming a Fixer is ongoing. Commit to continuous learning and development, staying open to new ideas, feedback, and opportunities for growth.

CHAPTER 18: BECOMING THE ULTIMATE FIXER

Final Thoughts:

Becoming a Fixer is about more than just acquiring a set of skills—it's about adopting a mindset that embraces change, innovation, and continuous improvement. As you apply the principles discussed in this book, you'll not only enhance your own capabilities but also contribute to the growth and success of the organisation.

My Mantra:

Every problem has a solution, you just have to be crazy enough to find it!

REFERENCES

Chapter 1: The Lost Art of the Generalist

Generalists vs. Specialists

1. **David Epstein's "Range: Why Generalists Triumph in a Specialized World"**: Epstein argues that generalists, who have a broad range of knowledge, often perform better in unpredictable environments compared to specialists.
   - Epstein, D. (2019). Range: Why generalists triumph in a specialized world. Penguin Random House.

2. **Generalists vs. Specialists in the Workforce**: An article from **The Economist** highlights how generalists are more resilient in times of economic uncertainty.
   - The Economist (2020). "Specialist or generalist? The economics of the two work styles".

Chapter 2: The Search for the Fixer

Project Managers as Fixers

1. **PMI's "Pulse of the Profession" Report**: This annual report from the Project Management Institute explores how project managers must adapt and exhibit traits of Fixers to drive success in volatile environments.
   - Project Management Institute (2020). Pulse of the Profession: What's Next for Project

Management.
2. **Transformational Leadership**: Research on transformational leadership indicates that leaders who are adaptable and strategic thinkers (i.e., Fixers) can have a significant positive impact on organisational performance.
   - Bass, B. M., & Avolio, B. J. (1994). Improving organisational effectiveness through transformational leadership. Sage Publications.

Chapter 3: T.E.A.L. Framework
Emotional Intelligence (EQ) and Leadership

1. **Daniel Goleman's Research on Emotional Intelligence**: Goleman's studies show that EQ is one of the key factors that distinguishes high-performing leaders, including those in Fixer roles.
   - Goleman, D. (1998). What makes a leader? Harvard Business Review.
2. **Trust and Transparency**: Research by **The Center for Creative Leadership** on trust-building in organisations shows that leaders who establish trust through transparent communication and consistency outperform those who don't.
   - Reina, D. S., & Reina, M. L. (2010). Trust and betrayal in the workplace: Building effective relationships in the organisation. Berrett-Koehler Publishers.
3. **Herbert Simon's Theory of Bounded Rationality**: Simon's research supports the need for quick, logical decision-making in environments of uncertainty.
   - Simon, H. A. (1979). Rational decision making in business organisations. American

Economic Review, 69(4), 493-513.

Chapter 4: Your Leadership Style
Transformational and Situational Leadership

1. **Bass and Avolio's Transformational Leadership Theory**: Transformational leaders, much like Fixers, inspire and motivate teams while driving organisational change.
    - Bass, B. M., & Avolio, B. J. (1990). The implications of transactional and transformational leadership for individual, team, and organisational development. Research in organisational Change and Development.

2. **Robert Greenleaf's Servant Leadership Theory**: Servant leaders prioritize the development and well-being of their teams, aligning with how Fixers foster trust and empower others.
    - Greenleaf, R. K. (1977). Servant leadership: A journey into the nature of legitimate power and greatness. Paulist Press.

Chapter 5: Decentralized Learning Theory
Informal and Decentralized Learning

1. **70:20:10 Model of Learning**: This model emphasizes that 70% of learning comes from job-related experiences, aligning with the Fixer's emphasis on on-the-job problem-solving.
    - Lombardo, M. M., & Eichinger, R. W. (1996). The Career Architect Development Planner. Lominger Limited.

2. **Jay Cross on Informal Learning**: Cross coined the term informal learning, showing how it happens outside

formal structures, through peer collaboration and self-directed work.
- **Cross, J. (2007). Informal Learning: Rediscovering the Natural Pathways That Inspire Innovation and Performance. Pfeiffer.**

Chapter 6: 0 to 100
Flow Theory and Peak Performance

1. **Mihaly Csikszentmihalyi's Research on Flow**: Flow theory shows how achieving deep focus can lead to increased productivity and creativity—core traits for Fixers.
   - **Csikszentmihalyi, M. (1990). Flow: The Psychology of Optimal Experience. Harper & Row.**

Chapter 7: Perception
Managing Internal and External Perception

1. **Erving Goffman's Work on Impression Management**: Goffman's foundational work on how individuals manage perceptions in social and professional contexts is key for Fixers who need to influence stakeholders.
   - **Goffman, E. (1959). The Presentation of Self in Everyday Life. Doubleday Anchor Books.**
2. **Tom Peters' Work on Personal Branding**: Peters' writings emphasize the importance of building and managing a personal brand, which aligns with the Fixer's need to manage both internal and external perception.
   - **Peters, T. (1997). "The Brand Called You." Fast Company Magazine.**
3. **Harvard Business Review on Perception Management**: This article discusses how leaders can shape perceptions

through deliberate action and communication, critical for Fixers navigating complex environments.
   - **Cuddy, A., Kohut, M., & Neffinger, J. (2013).** "Connect, Then Lead." Harvard Business Review.

Chapter 8: The Big Picture
Strategic Vision and Alignment

1. **Michael Porter's Competitive Strategy**: Porter's work on competitive advantage and alignment emphasizes the importance of linking short-term decisions to long-term strategy.
   - **Porter, M. E. (1985).** Competitive advantage: Creating and sustaining superior performance. Free Press.

Chapter 9: Blueprints to Scale
Scaling and Strategy

1. **Eric Ries' Lean Startup Methodology**: Ries emphasizes building, testing, and iterating ideas quickly, a core practice for scaling in the Fixer's toolkit.
   - **Ries, E. (2011).** The Lean Startup: How Today's Entrepreneurs Use Continuous Innovation to Create Radically Successful Businesses. Crown Publishing Group.
2. **SWOT Analysis**: A classic tool for strategic planning used to assess internal strengths and weaknesses and external opportunities and threats.
   - **Humphrey, A. S. (2005).** SWOT analysis for management consulting. SRI Alumni Association Newsletter.

Chapter 10: Precious Resource

Employee Well-Being and Engagement

1. **Gallup's State of the Global Workplace Report**: This report connects employee well-being and engagement with higher productivity, showing the critical link for Fixers to foster well-being in teams.
    - Gallup (2021). State of the Global Workplace.
2. **World Health organisation (WHO)** studies show that improving employee mental health can lead to significant productivity gains and reduction in absenteeism.
    - WHO (2020). Mental health in the workplace: Information sheet.

Chapter 11: Navigating Digital Transformation

Digital Transformation Research

1. **McKinsey & Company's Report on Digital Transformation**: This report outlines how digital tools must be aligned with organisational goals to drive transformation.
    - McKinsey & Company (2020). "How to restart your stalled digital transformation." McKinsey Quarterly.

Chapter 12: Inclusive Leadership and the Power of Diversity

Diversity and Inclusion in Leadership

1. **McKinsey's "Diversity Wins" Report**: This research shows that companies with diverse leadership teams

outperform their peers in profitability and innovation.
    - McKinsey & Company (2020). "Diversity Wins: How Inclusion Matters.".
2. **Harvard Business Review on Inclusive Leadership**: Studies show that inclusive leaders who foster psychological safety and embrace diverse perspectives are more successful.
    - Bourke, J., & Espedido, A. (2019). Why inclusive leaders are good for organisations, and how to become one. Harvard Business Review.

Chapter 13: Leading in Remote and Hybrid Work Environments

Remote Work Challenges and Solutions

1. **Buffer's "State of Remote Work" Report**: Provides insights into the challenges and benefits of remote work, including communication, collaboration, and productivity.
    - Buffer (2021). "State of Remote Work 2021".
2. **Gallup Report on Remote Work**: This study shows that remote workers can be highly productive if managed effectively with clear goals and communication.
    - Gallup (2021). "The Future of Remote Work: A Long-Term Look".

Chapter 14: Managing Mental Health and Well-Being

Mental Health in the Workplace

1. **APA's Report on Workplace Mental Health**: This report discusses the importance of promoting mental health and provides evidence that well-being initiatives

improve productivity.
      - **American Psychological Association (2019). Workplace Mental Health Survey Report**.
2. **Christina Maslach's Research on Burnout**: Maslach developed the widely used Maslach Burnout Inventory, which shows how burnout affects productivity and mental health.
      - **Maslach, C., & Jackson, S. E. (1981). The measurement of experienced burnout. Journal of Occupational behaviour, 2(2), 99-113.**

Chapter 15: Sustainability and Ethical Leadership

Ethical Leadership and Sustainability

1. **Treviño & Brown's Research on Ethical Leadership**: Their work demonstrates how ethical leadership promotes organisational trust and long-term sustainability.
      - **Treviño, L. K., & Brown, M. E. (2005). The role of leaders in influencing unethical behaviour in the workplace. Academy of Management Perspectives, 19(2), 69-81.**
2. **United Nations Global Compact (UNGC) Report on Sustainability**: This report outlines how businesses that integrate sustainability into their core strategies tend to perform better over time, both financially and in terms of brand reputation.
      - **United Nations Global Compact (2015). "Guide to Corporate Sustainability"**.
3. **McKinsey Report on Sustainability**: McKinsey found that companies with strong environmental, social, and governance (ESG) practices outperform their peers,

providing long-term financial value.
- McKinsey & Company (2020). "Five Ways That ESG Creates Value".

Chapter 16: Agile Leadership and Adaptability

Agile Leadership and the Iterative Process

1. **Scrum and Agile Methodology by Ken Schwaber and Jeff Sutherland:** Agile methodologies emphasize adaptability, rapid iteration, and cross-functional collaboration—all traits of a successful Fixer.
   - **Schwaber, K., & Sutherland, J. (2017). The Scrum Guide: The Definitive Guide to Scrum: The Rules of the Game.**

2. **Research on Agile Leadership:** This study outlines how agile leaders need to embrace flexibility, constant feedback, and rapid decision-making to drive innovation.
   - **Denning, S. (2018). "The age of agile: How smart companies are transforming the way work gets done." AMACOM.**

3. **Deloitte's Agile Enterprise Report:** Explores how businesses adopting agile methodologies outperform those with rigid structures in terms of innovation and adaptability.
   - **Deloitte (2021). "The Agile Enterprise: Reinventing the organisation for a Digital World".**

Chapter 17: Blueprints to Start

Ideation, Validation, and Startups

1. **Eric Ries' Lean Startup Methodology:** Ries advocates

for validating ideas through minimal viable products (MVPs) and continuous testing, a process essential for starting new ventures.
    - Ries, E. (2011). **The Lean Startup: How today's entrepreneurs use continuous innovation to create radically successful businesses.** Crown Publishing Group.
2. **Customer Discovery and Validation by Steve Blank**: This book provides detailed frameworks on how to validate business ideas using customer feedback, aligning with the Fixer's role in new ventures.
    - Blank, S. (2013). **The Four Steps to the Epiphany: Successful strategies for products that win.** K&S Ranch Publishing.
3. **Global Entrepreneurship Monitor (GEM) Report**: GEM provides annual insights into the success factors and challenges of startups globally, emphasizing the importance of validating ideas early.
    - Global Entrepreneurship Monitor (2020). **GEM 2019/2020 Global Report.**

Chapter 18: Becoming the Ultimate Fixer

Leadership Development and Case Studies

1. **Case Study on Ed Catmull's Leadership at Pixar**: Ed Catmull's leadership style is a classic example of a Fixer who transformed Pixar's operations through creative problem-solving and strategic thinking.
    - Catmull, E., & Wallace, A. (2014). **Creativity, Inc.: Overcoming the unseen forces that stand in the way of true inspiration.** Random House.
2. **Case Study on Sheryl Sandberg at Facebook**: Sandberg's approach to scaling Facebook through operational clarity and revenue generation has been widely studied

as an example of transformative leadership.
   - **Sandberg, S. (2013). Lean In: Women, work, and the will to lead. Alfred A. Knopf.**

3. **Case Study on Alan Mulally's Turnaround at Ford**: Mulally's leadership in turning around Ford without government assistance is a prime example of a Fixer's strategic thinking and resilience.
   - **Hoffman, B. (2012). American Icon: Alan Mulally and the fight to save Ford Motor Company. Crown Business.**

4. **Leadership Development Research**: Studies on continuous leadership development show that high-performing leaders continuously reflect, seek feedback, and evolve their approaches.
   - **Day, D. V. (2001). Leadership development: A review in context. The Leadership Quarterly, 11(4), 581-613.**

5. **Executive Coaching and Fixer Development**: Research on executive coaching emphasizes its role in helping leaders like Fixers refine their skills and continuously improve their impact.
   - **Grant, A. M., Curtayne, L., & Burton, G. (2009). Executive coaching enhances goal attainment, resilience, and workplace well-being: A randomized controlled study. The Journal of Positive Psychology, 4(5), 396-407.**

ABOUT THE AUTHOR

Teivian, the author of *Becoming a Fixer*, has spent over a decade mastering the art of adaptability, leadership, and problem-solving across a diverse range of industries. From e-learning to technology and management consulting, Teivian's career has been defined by stepping into complex situations and providing clear, strategic solutions to drive growth and transformation. As a Fixer, Teivian has become known for an ability to navigate uncertainty, identify opportunities for improvement, and align teams around a shared vision for success.

Starting with early roles in government and the e-learning sector, Teivian quickly learned that the key to thriving in any environment is adaptability—moving from rigid structures to more dynamic, innovation-driven industries. With a passion for creating order from chaos, Teivian was soon recognised for the ability to lead teams through change, build cross-functional collaboration, and foster cultures that prioritize innovation and growth.

Throughout his career, Teivian has emphasized the importance of peer-to-peer learning, ethical leadership, and sustainability, which are central themes in *Becoming a Fixer*. By applying practical frameworks like T.E.A.L. (Trust, Emotional Quotient, Action, Logic), Teivian has consistently driven measurable improvements, whether in scaling startups or transforming established organizations. Known for being an analytical thinker with a hands-on approach, Teivian believes that success lies not just in solving problems but in continuously learning, evolving, and challenging the status quo.

Teivian's experience has shaped a belief in the power of versatile leadership—adapting leadership styles to suit different situations and people—and in the need for ethical decision-making that drives both business success and positive social impact. Whether navigating digital transformations, driving sustainability initiatives, or mentoring teams to foster a culture of continuous improvement, Teivian's work is focused on empowering individuals and organizations to unlock their full potential.

Through *Becoming a Fixer*, Teivian shares the strategies, insights, and real-world examples that have defined his career, offering readers a practical guide to becoming the problem-solving leader every organization needs.

www.ingramcontent.com/pod-product-compliance
Lightning Source LLC
Chambersburg PA
CBHW070351230526
45471CB00006B/2510